D0833738

Assessing Children in Need and Their Parents

The PACTS series: *Parent, Adolescent and Child Training Skills*

Assessing Children in Need and Their Parents

by
Martin Herbert

BPS BOOKS THE BRITISH PSYCHOLOGICAL SOCIETY

First published in 1996 by BPS Books (The British Psychological Society), St Andrews House, 48 Princess Road East, Leicester LE1 7DR, UK.

A catalogue record for this book is available from the British Library.

ISBN 1 85433 192 2

Typeset by Ralph Footring, Derby.

Printed in Great Britain by Stanley L. Hunt Printers Ltd., Rushden, Northants.

Contents

APPENDICES

Assessing children in need and their parents

Introduction

This guide is specifically about the assessment of children in need. Under today's legislation, a child is taken to be in need if (a) s/he is unlikely to achieve or maintain, or to have the opportunity of achieving or maintaining, a reasonable standard of health or development without the provision for him/her of specified services by a local authority; or (b) s/he is likely to be significantly impaired, or further impaired, without provision of such services; or (c) s/he is disabled. A child is disabled if s/he is blind, deaf or dumb, suffers from mental disorder of any kind, or is substantially handicapped by illness, injury, or congenital deformity.

Aims

The aims of this guide are to provide practitioners with:

1. an introduction to the concept of *children in need* (the *need* dealt with here may be for the child to be protected from abuse; for special education and care; for other interventions by the helping professions and the community);
2. a guide to the meaning of 'significant harm', as defined in the Children Act, 1989;
3. guidelines, checklists and proforma for assessing the quality of child care, and risky situations.

It should be noted that while the underlying principles of the Children Act, 1989, are the same, there are minor differences in the Children Order (as it is known) in N. Ireland. The Children (Scotland) Act overlaps considerably with English legislation.

Objectives

When you have read this book you should be able to:

1. be familiar with the main requirements for assessing children in need;

2. describe the major forms of child abuse;
3. describe and assess parental responsibility and responsiveness;
4. appreciate the impact of a child in need on parents and family life;
5. describe criteria for health and development;
6. define significant harm;
7. describe briefly special educational needs and disability.

Part I: Children in need of protection

Definition

The definitions of child abuse recommended as criteria for registration throughout England and Wales by the Departments of Health, Education and Science, the Home Office and Welsh Office (1991) in their joint document *Working Together Under the Children Act, 1989* are as follow:

Neglect. The persistent or severe neglect of a child, or the failure to protect a child from exposure to any kind of danger, including cold and starvation, or extreme failure to carry out important aspects of care, resulting in the significant impairment of the child's health or development, including non-organic failure to thrive.

Physical injury. Actual or likely physical injury to a child, or failure to prevent physical injury (or suffering) to a child, including deliberate poisoning, suffocation and Munchausen's syndrome by proxy.

Sexual abuse. Actual or likely sexual exploitation of a child or adolescent. The child may be dependent and/or developmentally immature. Sexual exploitation represents the involvement of dependent, developmentally immature children and adolescents in sexual activities they do not truly comprehend, to which they are unable to give informed consent or that violate social taboos of family roles.

Emotional abuse. Actual or likely severe adverse effect on the emotional and behavioural development of a child caused by persistent or severe emotional ill-treatment or rejection. All abuse involves some emotional ill-treatment. This category is used where it is the main or sole form of abuse.

Mixed categories are also recorded, which register more than one type of abuse and/or neglect occurring to a child. This is especially important when considering 'organised abuse', which is defined in the same document (op. cit., page 38) as: 'Abuse which may involve a number of abusers, a number of abused children and young people and often encompass different forms of abuse. It involves, to a greater or lesser extent an element of organisation'.

Children at risk

Since 1990, the Department of Health in England has assessed the number of children and young persons on Child Protection Registers. The estimates are based on annual statistical returns from all 109 Local Government Authorities. Between 1993 to 1994, 45,800 children were the subject of initial child protection case conferences and 62 per cent of them were placed on the register. The overall rate for various age groups on the register in England was 3.2 children per thousand under 18 years of age, representing 34,900 names. The highest rates were found in very young children under five years (4 to 5 per 1000).

In all, on 31 March 1994, 17,400 girls and boys and 100 unborn children in England were considered to require protection from maltreatment and one in five (21 per cent) of them were in care. Of the 7,500 children in care at this time, 4,800 were placed with foster parents and 1,000 were living in residential homes or hostels.

Prevalence

Some researchers claim that the new cases of child abuse and neglect which are reported (the *incidence rate*), represent only a small proportion of the *actual* number of maltreated children in society at any one time (the *prevalence rate*). As nine out of ten children are hit by their parents it is suggested that a high proportion of child abuse and neglect may go undetected.

Parental responsibility

In order to raise a child well one ought not try to be a perfect parent, as much as one should not expect one's child to be, or to become, a perfect individual. Perfection is not within the grasp of ordinary human beings ... But it is quite possible to be a good enough parent. . . .

Bruno Bettelheim (1987)

The concept of parental responsibility is enshrined in legislation, notably in the Children Act. It refers to 'all the rights, duties, powers, responsibilities and authority which by law a parent of a child has in relation to the child and his property' [s.3(1)].

The new concept of *parental responsibility* seeks to balance the rights and duties of parents with the welfare of the child. With the birth (or adoption) of the first child, the tasks of the parents, the roles they occupy, their orientation toward the future, all change profoundly. Taking care of young children is likely to be overwhelming for some parents; it requires considerable maturity to shift one's orientation from being mainly adult-centred to being primarily child-centred. The responsibility of a total commitment to a baby, especially for young parents used to having their freedom and responsibility only for themselves, may seem awesome and, sometimes, depressing. The inevitable changes will alter the parents' relationship and may place stresses upon it until a new equilibrium can be established in their lives. The heightened emotional intimacy and interdependence of members of small, intimate nuclear families can place a great burden on parents, most particularly on the mother.

Parental responsiveness (see *Appendices IV* and *V*)

Responsibility as parents goes hand-in-hand with parental responsiveness – that is, caring attitudes towards a child. More than the protection and nurturance of a helpless infant is at stake. There is a further responsibility – the all-important transmission of culture. This cannot be left to chance. The welfare of the individual and the continuity of the culture depend upon there being a satisfactory means of inducting the new generation into society's mores, attitudes and skills to ensure that they, in turn, will satisfactorily hand on the culture and assume the role of another generation of parents.

Part II: Children in need of special education/care

Contending with a disability (see Lewis, 1987)

The Children Act places a clear, positive and separate duty on local authorities (the local Social Services Departments) to provide services with the purpose of:

➤ minimizing the effect on children with disabilities in the area of their disabilities; and

➤ giving such children the chance to lead lives which are as normal as possible (para. 6, Schedule 2).

Table 1 can be used as a preliminary check to indicate the presence or absence of disability, but, of course, the relevant specialists will have to be consulted in the case of a formal assessment.

Special educational needs

The 1981 Education Act refers to a separate category of children with special educational needs. The Act gives parents the right to take part in assessments of their child and in its decisions regarding school placement. The Warnock Report that preceded the Act spoke of parents as partners. Following an assessment (notably by educational psychologists), a *statement of special educational need* was provided for each child between the ages of two and 19, setting out the educational provision for the child as required (see Herbert, 1993).

Table 1.　Disability checklist (from Herbert, 1993)

Hearing

moderate to severe　　hearing difficulties even with hearing aids; has, or is likely to have, persisting difficulty with language and communication sufficient to impair development.

profound　　little or no hearing, with little or no benefit from hearing aids.

Vision

moderate to severe　　partially sighted, visual difficulties sufficient to impair everyday activities and/or development despite the use of aids.

profound　　blind, no useful vision.

Speech and/or language

moderate to severe　　difficulties communicating through speech and language, and, as a result, unable to participate in the normal activities of a child of their age.

profound　　no meaningful speech or language, therefore unlikely to use speech as the primary means of communication.

Physical

moderate to severe　　physical difficulty (for example, motor) or chronic illness resulting in long-term impairment of health or development, even with the provision of drugs, diet or aids.

profound　　difficulties with all basic functions, of such severity that assistance is likely to be required.

Learning

moderate to severe　　a permanent learning impairment sufficient to prevent the child from fulfilling roles or performing activities which are generally understood to be within the capacity of children of that age and cultural background.

profound　　profound or multiple learning difficulties.

Behavioural and emotional

moderate to severe　　emotional and/or behavioural difficulties likely to be long-term, and be such as to impair the quality of the child's life, resulting in underachievement in normal social contexts (for example, school or workplace), with failure of social development and integration.

profound　　emotional and/or behavioural difficulties likely to be so severe in the long-term that they seriously impair the quality of the child's life, resulting in inability to function in normal social contexts or constituting a risk to themselves or others.

Part III: Children in need and their families

The impact of children with special needs

Children who are disabled (intellectually and/or physically), or chronically ill, are more likely to have behavioural and emotional problems than healthy children. This puts an additional strain on parents struggling to cope with the disability/illness in its own right. Hilton Davis, in his valuable guide *Counselling Parents of Children with Chronic Illness and Disability* (1993), points out how each disability/disease presents specific problems to the child and family.

> *When children are hurt, ill or disabled, they need physical and personal attention, and this has consequences for all members of the family. At a relatively trivial level, one of the parents has to stop cooking, reading or watching television to see to the child, to cuddle him/her or kiss a bruise better. If the child is sick, parents become worried, arrangements have to be made to look after her/him while one parent takes the other children to school, or they have to make time to go to the G.P. Time may be lost from work, and the other children lose attention. Such consequences are a routine part of family life but, in chronic disease, they become a way of life. Anxiety may be the norm, outside commitments may be impossible and childcare duties are increased, including appointments with professionals and even periods away from home for hospital admissions.*

The family

Davis describes how parents are profoundly affected by illness in their children, with as many as 33 per cent of parents of children with cancer, even in remission, having such severe depression and anxiety that they require professional help. In a study conducted by Davis with one of his students, 31 per cent of mothers of children with diabetes were found to have stress levels that would have benefited from a professional mental health intervention.

Communication and relationship problems are reflected in increased marital distress, sometimes in divorce. There is evidence of

increased disturbance in siblings, including irritability, social with-
drawal, jealousy and guilt, academic under-achievement, behaviour
problems, anxiety, and low self-esteem. A major problem is the
disturbance of their social relationships, especially with their parents.
They tend to feel neglected in comparison with the disabled or
chronically ill child.

It is plain to see that the social context – the family unit – cannot
be overlooked in one's rightful concern about, and priority-giving to,
the child with special needs.

Assessing 'children in need'

Children in need

Each child should be assessed in terms of their:

➢ *physical well-being and physical care* (see *Appendix VII* and the health
  and development questionnaire in *Appendix IX*);
➢ *mental health*;
➢ *social and intellectual development*;
➢ *emotional development* (the quality of parental care) and *behaviour* (see
  Appendix VI).

Each professional should refer to their own practice tools and to
their agency guidance.

Criteria for assessing health and development

All criteria relate to a child similar in age, gender and from a similar
cultural, racial and religious background.

➢ *Reasonable standard:* a child is determined as not achieving or
  maintaining a 'reasonable standard' of health or development when
  their conduct, presentation or care detrimentally sets them apart.

➢ *Significant impairment:* the health and development of a child is to be
  regarded as 'significantly impaired' where there is objective evidence
  (developmental assessments, child protection events, and so on) that
  the child's development is being adversely and avoidably impaired
  through lack of parenting skills/resources.

➢ *Disability* (see checklist in *Table 1*): is there visual impairment, hearing
  impairment, serious communication difficulties, substantial handicap stemming from illness, injury or congenital conditions?

> ➤ *Significant risk*: whether a child is 'significantly at risk' needs to be determined by a child protection case conference. Some children may be at risk, and, in turn, 'in need', although there is no evidence that they are not achieving or maintaining a 'reasonable standard of health and development'.

> ➤ *Significant harm*: a child's health and/or development is being 'significantly harmed' through acts of omission or commission on the part of the parent(s)/carer(s) or because the child is beyond parental control (see page 15).

> ➤ *Development* means physical, intellectual, emotional, social or behavioural development and *health* means physical or mental health.

In this last item lies a major part of the professional's dilemma. What is a reasonable standard of development? And what constitutes physical or mental health, let alone their impairment? The word 'need' is also difficult to define precisely! It appears in the Children Act within the list of terms defining the child's welfare; that is, his/her 'physical, emotional and educational needs'. Masson (1990) notes that the emphasis should be on an *objective* assessment of the needs of the individual child, but there is a danger that subjectivity in the form of preference for particular life styles might be introduced here. After all, we often owe allegiance to, in the sense of valuing, the way that we were brought up, and to the traditions of the culture we belong to.

We can never overestimate the difficulties faced by social and health service practitioners, notably social workers and health visitors, in making the agonizing decisions that society burdens them with; they have to balance the needs and safety of children and the needs and rights of parents. Theirs is only too often a situation in which they always lose: they are scapegoats when things go tragically amiss (fortunately, rarely) and they are unacknowledged when they get things right.

Understandably, the hard-pressed social worker cannot afford to be as complacent as the scientist in risking what the statisticians call 'Type II errors' — that is, denying relationships which actually exist because of a cautious attitude to evidence. Whilst it may be understandable that s/he errs on the side of making 'Type I errors' (asserting relationships falsely) in a fraught area like child abuse, the implications of Type I errors may also be harmful to clients. Interventions which are, at best, ineffectual, and at worst, demoralizing, may be the cost. In any event there *are* several problems connected with the collating of 'evidence' and the formulations (theories/judgements/predictions /recommendations) that flow from the information and data.

It is important to marshal the reasons given for choosing particular judgements and decisions. *Rational* arguments for a point of view are required, not personal sentiment or prejudice. Professionals carrying out an assessment obviously need a sound empirical knowledge base for their recommendations and decisions.

Objectives

It is important to be clear about what questions are being posed in the assessment; what is its purpose and, therefore, your objectives. The Children Act uses the concept of 'reasonable parents'. In referring to care orders, Section 31 specifies that the care must be 'what it would be reasonable to expect a parent to give'. One is reminded here of the concept of a 'good enough' parent – a notion that sounds plausible but which is notoriously difficult to define, and therefore difficult to assess (see also p. 17).

Methods of assessment

If an assessment of these matters is to be trusted, then the methods or indicators used, and their application, should meet certain criteria.

➤ They should have the appropriate breadth and specificity of coverage. Observations, for example, should be of a *representative sample* of the client's behaviour occurring in specified situations.

➤ They should provide indicators or measures that are *fair.* (This point is related to the preceding one.) The assessment should not apply to a biased or narrow aspect of the clients' activities or attitudes, nor should one use tests or questions that are culture-bound (ethnocentric) and which therefore discriminate unfairly against particular persons.

➤ They should provide *accurate* indicators or measures. This means that they should be *reliable,* and, if circumstances allow, *repeatable.* They should also be translated into precise statements and descriptions as opposed to vague, global terminology.

➤ They should provide indicators or measures that are *relevant.* Relevance is critical if assessments are to be valid. In other words, assessments should measure or indicate what they purport to measure/indicate.

➤ They should be *practical* to use. There is little point in using unwieldy, time-consuming, esoteric methods.

➤ They should be *ethical*. This is a *sine qua non* of all one's practice.

Part IV: Assessing parenting

When is a child being harmed?

The professional may have a nagging concern about a child who is failing to thrive or cope and/or about the parents who may be ignorant or unwilling to face up to possible harm to their child because of the state of his/her health or development. *At least* the professional must have 'reasonable cause to suspect that the child is suffering or is likely to suffer, significant harm' [s.43(1)(a)]. For example, the needs of children who are potentially at risk are of two kinds:

1. *survival* functions such as the need for food, shelter and physical care; and
2. *psychosocial* functions, including the child's requirements of love, security, attention, new experiences, acceptance, education, praise, recognition and belongingness.

Infants and children, if they are to survive, must also acquire vast amounts of information about the environment they inhabit. One of the main objectives of this training by the parents is the preparation of children for their future. It is doubtful whether any child, in our far from ideal world, has all of his/her individual needs satisfied by parents. This, in part, is why the term 'good enough parenting' has entered the professional vocabulary.

Harm

The concept of harm is defined in Section 31 (9) in Part IV of the Children Act to mean ill-treatment *or* the impairment of physical or mental health or development. 'Development', as already noted (p. 10), refers to physical, intellectual, emotional, social or behavioural development, and 'ill treatment' includes sexual abuse and forms of ill-treatment which are not only physical (see *Appendix I*). Impairment of health or development therefore also covers *any* case of neglect: poor nutrition, low standards of hygiene, poor emotional care through failure to seek treatment for an illness or condition.

Whatever the nature of the harm, the court has to decide whether the harm is, in itself, significant (see *Appendix II*). This relates to the seriousness of the harm *and* its implications for the child. The court must also consider whether the child is suffering harm *currently* or whether s/he is *likely* to suffer it. Likelihood, according to White (1991), means that harm is higher than a mere possibility, but not as high as 'more likely than not'. Section 31 of the Act requires the court to be satisfied, before making a care or supervision order and before applying the principles in Section 1 of the Act, that certain criteria (referred to as *threshold criteria*) exist in the child's circumstances (see *Figure A*).

The central concept of the criteria is harm. But even if the threshold criteria are met, the court may still decide not to make a care or supervision order. It has to take into account the welfare checklist in *Table 2* (p. 16) and, in particular, the range of orders available to the court, which include the orders under Section 8 of the Act. These orders can be made *whether or not* the threshold criteria are satisfied.

The question that still begs an answer is that very difficult one: *at what point can it be said that a child is actually being harmed by the neglect of needs or the presence of unskilled, insensitive or inexperienced parenting **to a significant extent**?* After all, it is not the cases of explicitly malicious abuse or extreme neglect that create the agonizing debates about what constitutes harm. The harm being done is obvious. It is the more subtle and ambiguous consequences for the child's well-being flowing from parental ignorance, inexperience, emotional inadequacies or lack of resourcefulness, that evade confident classification.

It is important to remember that where it is a question of whether harm suffered by a child is *significant,* his/her health or development is 'compared with that which could reasonably be expected of a similar child' [s.31(10)]. A similar child is defined as a child with the same physical attributes as the child concerned, not a child of the same background. But this ignores the fact that social and environmental factors contribute very significantly to what can be achieved. The definition of significant harm crops up in various places in the Act: in child assessment orders under Section 43, emergency protection orders under Section 44, the police power to remove a child under Section 46, the local authority's duty to investigate under Section 47, and detention in secure accommodation under Section 25.

The child assessment order

When an assessment is necessary and the parents/caregivers refuse to agree, the applicant may seek a child assessment order lasting up

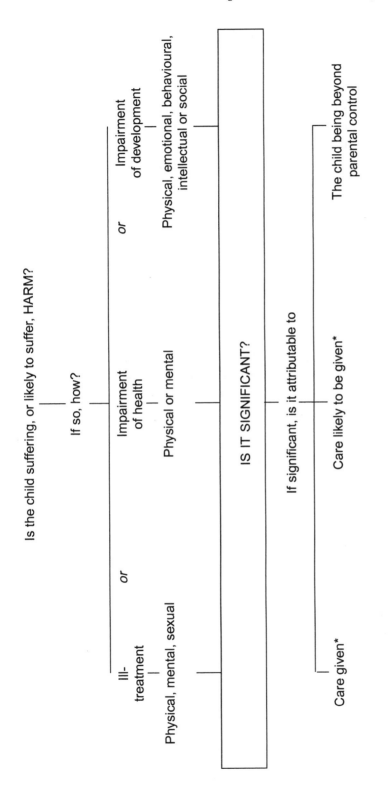

*Not what it would be reasonable to expect a parent to give to the child.

Figure A. The threshold criteria for assessing 'significant harm' (adapted from White, 1991).

to seven days [s.43]. A proposal to apply for a child assessment order [s.43(1)], and the arrangements to be discussed with the court for the assessment, could be considered at a case conference according to local child protection procedures. The person who has expressed concern about the child to the Local Authority and Social Services Department or to the National Society for the Prevention of Cruelty to Children (NSPCC), the only agencies which can apply for a child assessment order, will have to contribute to the conference's considerations.

The child's parents or carers should always be told that a child assessment order may be applied for if they persist in refusing to co-operate. They should also be informed of the legal effect and detailed implications of the order, and the court procedure that will be followed. Parents will also need information about the purpose of an assessment.

The child's wishes and feelings

Communicating with the child is emphasized, as his/her views in proceedings are seen to be of great significance. The welfare checklist (*Table 2*) to which the court is to have regard in reaching decisions about the child is headed by the child's wishes and feelings.

Table 2   Welfare checklist [s.1(3)]

The following items must be assessed for Court proceedings:

(a)   the ascertainable wishes and feelings of the child concerned (considered in the light of the child's age and understanding);
(b)   the child's physical, emotional and educational needs;
(c)   the likely effect on the child of any change in circumstances;
(d)   the child's age, sex, background and any characteristics that the court considers relevant;
(e)   any harm the child has suffered, or is at risk of suffering;
(f)   how capable each of the child's parents, and any other person in relation to whom the court considers the question to be relevant, is of meeting the child's needs;
(g)   the range of powers available to the court under this Act in the proceedings in question.

When a court determines any question with respect to the upbringing of a child, it has regard, in particular, to the ascertainable wishes and feelings of the child concerned (considered in the light of his/her age and understanding). Thus there is a greater emphasis than in earlier legislation on consulting children and finding out their views.

So how does one find out what the child wants? As with all persons, the major methods used are *observation, questioning* and giving a *sympathetic 'hearing'*. *Interviewing,* because of the opportunity it gives to 'ask them', 'question them' and, by no means least, 'listen to them', becomes a prime instrument of assessment, investigation, intervention and evaluation. *Verbal report*, based upon clinical conversations, may be a fairly good predictor of real-life behaviour, but it can also be very misleading, and therefore, unreliable. Do not rely entirely on it (and that means on the interview) for your data. Clients, including children, may not notice things, may misperceive events, or may forget significant details and emphasize irrelevant points.

Embarrassment or guilt may lead to errors of commission and omission in information-giving. If the crucial behaviour consists of overlearned responses, the client may be quite unaware ('unconscious') of his/her actions. So go and look for yourself and/or train clients to observe, so that you can see things through their informed eyes. Even then, you may observe patterns of behaviour which misrepresent the 'true' state of affairs. Your 'snapshots' may be contaminated by an observer effect; people and situations change as you observe them. Clients may play a part, knowing full well what you are looking for. The meaning of behaviours may not be apparent if you are not fully aware of the nuances of context and background of certain relationships and interactions. You may over-generalize observations to make 'traits', 'tendencies' or 'deep-seated motives' out of what are merely situation-specific actions.

Assessing parent–child relationships in high-risk families

According to Browne (in Browne and Herbert, 1996), there are six important aspects to assessing high-risk parent–child relationships and determining how safe the child is.

1. The evaluation of caretaker's knowledge and attitudes to parenting the child.
2. Parental perceptions of the child's behaviour and the child's perceptions of the parent.
3. The quality of parenting.
4. The observation of parent–child interaction and behaviour.

5.   The quality of child to parent attachment.
6.   Parental emotions and responses to stress.

I will now consider the first three.

Knowledge and attitudes to child rearing

Research suggests that abusing and non-abusing families have different attitudes about child development. For example, abusers tend to have unrealistic and distorted expectations of their children's abilities. They may have much higher expectations and this influences discipline and punishment. They may have unrealistic beliefs that babies should be able to sit alone at 12 weeks and take their first steps at 40 weeks. More importantly, they may expect their infants to be able to recognize wrong-doing at 52 weeks. Not surprisingly, a significant proportion of sexual and physical abusive incidents involve fruitless attempts by parents to force a child to behave in a manner that is beyond the child's developmental limitations.

Research also suggests that one of the differences between abusing and non-abusing parents is that the abusing group sees child rearing as a simple, rather than a complex, task. Many of them show a lack of awareness of their child's abilities and needs.

Parental perceptions of child behaviour

Abusing parents tend to have more negative conceptions of their children's behaviour than non-abusing parents: they perceive their children to be more irritable and demanding. This may be related to the fact that abused children are more likely to have health problems, and eating or sleeping (or other behavioural) disturbances. Alternatively, it may be a direct result of their unrealistic expectations.

The quality of parenting (see *Appendices III–VIII*)

Parental responsiveness is a major element in assessing the quality of parenting. It is a complex and many-sided phenomenon, but there are at least three different elements which make for what one might assess to be sensitive responsiveness: the tendency of the parent to react *promptly, consistently*, and *appropriately,* to their offspring. A social worker or health visitor would be concerned if parents continually failed to react in these ways in response to their child's hunger, pain, crying or other communications and actions.

The interactions between parents and children (particularly the early ones) are of crucial significance in the child's development. And parenting is not simply a matter of being *reactive;* it is also about being *proactive*: initiating play, pre-empting accidents and facilitating learning by imaginative, resourceful care. Personal factors can interfere with these intricate processes. To take an extreme case, a mother suffering from depression may find it difficult to 'tune in' to her child in a sufficiently sensitive manner to be able to construct with him/her a mutually beneficial and stimulating sequence of interaction.

It is worth noting that although society delegates its most crucial functions to the family, there is little formal education or training offered to would-be parents; even the informal learning and experience once available to older children caring for younger siblings in large families, or the help from experienced members of the extended family and from relatives living nearby, may not be available to the relatively small and isolated modern nuclear family.

Child care practices are subject to fashions, not to say fads. It has been generally assumed that it matters a great deal how the infant is handled, and that unless reared 'correctly', the child's future could be blighted. The plain fact is that, despite much study, there is little hard evidence concerning the relationship between *specific* early child-rearing practices and subsequent personality development. Thus, we do not really know how particularities such as breast feeding or bottle feeding compare as regards their psychological consequences, or whether indeed, they make any difference. Likewise, we cannot be sure whether on-demand feeding is, or is not, better than feeding at fixed intervals, and we do not know whether early or late weaning makes a difference to the child's personality development. Indeed, the evidence suggests that one of the crucial features of child rearing is the general social climate in the home – the attitudes, expectations and feelings of the parents which provide the backdrop to the specific methods of child care and training which they use. Parents who do what they and the community to which they belong believe is right for the child are the most effective parents.

The evidence suggests that in a broad sense these parents attempt to direct their child's activities in a rational manner determined by the issues involved in particular disciplinary situations. They encourage verbal give-and-take and share with the child the reasoning behind their policy. They value both the child's self-expression and his/her respect for authority, work and the like. The evidence, according to Diana Baumrind (1989), points to a synthesis and balancing of strongly opposing forces of tradition and innovation, divergence and convergence, accommodation and assimilation, co-operation and independent expression, tolerance and principled intractability. She calls this 'authoritative' (*not* authoritarian) parenting.

Democratic parenting

MacKenzie (1993) describes the authoritative parent's so-called 'democratic approach' as follows.

Parents' beliefs

➤ Children are capable of solving problems on their own.
➤ Children should be given choices and allowed to learn from the consequences of their choices.
➤ Encouragement is an effective way to motivate co-operation.

Power and control

➤ Children are given only as much power and control as they can handle responsibly.

Problem-solving process

➤ Co-operative.
➤ Win–win (child and parent win).
➤ Based on mutual respect.
➤ Children are active participants in the problem-solving process.

What children learn

➤ Responsibility.
➤ Co-operation.
➤ Independence.
➤ Respect for rules and authority.
➤ Self-control.

How children respond

➤ More co-operation.
➤ Less limit testing.

➤ Resolve problems on their own.
➤ Regard parents' words seriously.

Parenting skills

The Children Act describes parents' ability to raise their child to moral, physical and emotional health. This demands a series of far-from-simple skills – part common sense, part intuition and part empathy (the ability to see things from another's point of view). All parents should provide for the basic survival needs of their children, namely safety, shelter, space (which includes space to play, and particularly for older children, privacy), food, income, physical care and health care. The child's physical care can be rated for its adequacy in the checklist in *Appendix VII*. Responsible parents also provide love, security, attention, new experiences, acceptance, education, praise and recognition in order to meet their children's vital psychosocial needs. There is a checklist in *Appendix VI* which can be used to assess the quality of parental emotional care.

A particularly difficult task is to encourage those feelings that come readily to most parents, but which are absent or distorted in a few. In the way that success breeds success and failure breeds failure, good parenting facilitates good parenting in the next generation, and poor parenting generates poor parenting. Fortunately, when it comes to the last part of that 'rule', there are, as with most aspects of child rearing, many exceptions.

Parent to child attachment (bonding)

The question of sensitive or insensitive responsiveness has been linked, in part, with the quality of the emotional 'bond' or 'attachment' that forms between the parent and baby (see *Appendices IV* and *V*) . The infant's survival depends upon a loving and long-term commitment by adult caregivers. Social workers and health visitors are on the lookout for signs of rejection, neglect and abuse – in other words, emotional abuse. This type of abuse can make children believe that they are worthless and that their very existence makes their parents unhappy. The child may be ignored, there may be inadequate physical care, the child may lack stimulation, physical contact, security. The child is thus denied emotional warmth and love as well as protection, support and discipline. Parents' negative attitudes may lead to abusive

threats, constant criticism and scapegoating. With older children, this is sometimes accompanied by ridicule and denigration of all the child's efforts to please. Some apply the term 'emotional abuse' also to over-protection of the kind that inhibits the child's progress toward maturity and dependency by cossetting and 'infantilizing' him/her.

The concept of emotional abuse is in danger of being over-inclusive and far too vague. It is therefore an advantage to have more tangible indicators to pinpoint its presence.

Indicator 1: entails punishment of positive 'operant' behaviour such as smiling, mobility, manipulation;

Indicator 2: is behaviour which results in discouragement of parent–infant bonding (for example, pushing children away every time they seek proximity, comfort and affection);

Indicator 3: involves the punishment of self-esteem as when parents endlessly criticize their child;

Indicator 4: is parental behaviour leading to the punishing of those interpersonal skills (for example, friendliness) which are vital for acceptance in environments outside the home, for example, school, peer groups.

It should not be forgotten that emotional abuse is also associated with physical and sexual abuse.

Helping parents

When things do go wrong, as sometimes happens when a temperamentally difficult infant or a child with a physical or mental disability makes heavy demands on parents, help is available. Many parents can be trained in the necessary skills in child care and behaviour management. More often than not they have skills they're not even aware of. To this end every family can make use of its combined store of skills so that members can usefully share and learn from each other (see Herbert, 1993). Behavioural parent training groups, conducted in a collaborative manner, are particularly effective (see Webster-Stratton and Herbert, 1994).

References

Baumrind, D. (1989). Rearing competent children. In: W. Damon (Ed.) *Child Development Today and Tomorrow*. San Francisco: Jossey-Bass.

Bettelheim, B. (1987). *A Good Enough Parent*.

Browne, K. and Herbert, M. (1996). *Preventing Family Violence*. Chichester: Wiley.

Davis, H. (1993). *Counselling Parents of Children with Chronic Illness and Disability*. Leicester: BPS Books (The British Psychological Society).

Departments of Health, Education and Science, Home Office and Welsh Office (1991). *Working Together Under the Children Act, 1989*. London: HMSO.

Herbert, M. (1993). *Working with Children and the Children Act*. Leicester: BPS Books (The British Psychological Society).

Kellmer Pringle, M. (1975). *The Needs of Children*.

Lewis, V. (1987). *Development and Handicap*. Oxford: Basil Blackwell.

MacKenzie, R.J. (1993). *Setting Limits*. Rocklin, C.A.: Prima Publishing.

Masson, J. (1990). *The Children Act 1989: Text and Commentary*. London: Sweet and Maxwell.

Webster-Stratton, C. and Herbert, M. (1994). *Troubled Families – Problem Children: A Collaborative Approach* Chichester: Wiley.

White, R. (1991). Examining the threshold criteria. In: M. Adcock, R. White and A. Hollows (Eds) *Significant Harm: Its Management and Outcome*. Croydon: Significant Publications.

Further reading

Department of Health and Social Services, Office of Law Reform (1995). *Introduction to the Children (NI) Order 1995*. Northern Ireland: HSMO.

Eisenberg, N. (Ed.) (1995). *Social Development*. London: Sage.

Iwaniec, D. (1995). *The Emotionally Abused and Neglected Child: Identification, Assessment and Intervention*. Chichester: Wiley.

Jordan, C. and Franklin, C. (1995). *Clinical Assessment for Social Workers*. Chicago: Lyceum Press.

Sluckin, W., Herbert, M. and Sluckin, A. (1983). *Maternal Bonding*. Oxford: Basil Blackwell.

Sutton, C. (1994). *Social Work, Community Work and Psychology*. Leicester: BPS Books (The British Psychological Society).

Appendices: Assessing parenting and children's needs

Forms and checklists follow; they are designed for ratings and evaluations based upon observations made, and questions asked, by yourself as caseworker and/or the self-report of the client. They are not meant to replace your agency's assessment instruments.

In a case where you are making your own judgements based upon observation, it is critical to reach a conclusion only after seeing a fair, that is, *representative*, sample of your client's behaviour in different settings and circumstances.

It is important to appreciate that the rating scales and questionnaires designed for use with clients do not provide definitive 'diagnostic' statements about clients and/or their problems. This is especially the case in the areas of child abuse and depression. Nor do the ratings or frequency tallies imply test scores of the kind that are obtained from personality or IQ tests. In other words, they are not strictly speaking numerical scales, that is to say, precise quantitative measures. They are designed to help you avoid 'fuzzy', global judgements by making finer assessments which can act as (and should be regarded as) guides only, clues to possible problems (for example, extremely high or low counts) and disorders (unusual or bizarre patterns). They are screening devices, the first stage in the search for further evidence, and they also provide 'markers' that will allow you to monitor change in your clients over periods of time. As such they are individualized (not normative or nomothetic) devices allowing you to indicate by observation or self-report, a person's behaviours, attitudes, feelings, relative to him/herself.

Throughout your assessment ask yourself:

➤ Is the child's adaptive behaviour appropriate to his/her age, intelligence, cultural context and social situation?
➤ Is the environment making reasonable demands of the child?
➤ Is the environment satisfying the crucial needs of the child, that is, the needs that are vital at his/her particular stage of development?

Appendix I: Forms of maltreatment

From Browne and Herbert (1996).

Abuse

Physical abuse

The infliction or threat of physical pain and/or injury, for example, pushing, slapping, hitting, hair-pulling, biting, arm-twisting, kicking, punching, hitting with objects, burning, stabbing, shooting, poisoning and so on. Forced coercion and physical restraint.

Sexual abuse

Sexual contact without consent, any exploitive or coercive sexual contact including fondling, intercourse, oral or anal sodomy, attacks on the sexual parts of the body. Involuntary viewing of sexual imagery or activity and treating someone in a sexually derogatory manner.

Psychological (mental abuse)

The infliction of mental anguish by controlling and limiting access to friends, school and work. Forced isolation and imprisonment. Involuntary witness to violent imagery or activity. Intimidation, using fear of physical harm or harm to others. Use of menacing, blackmail, suicide threats and harassment. Destruction of pets and property.

Emotional abuse

Regular criticism, humiliation, denigration, insults, put-downs, name calling and other attempts to undermine self-image and sense of worth.

Material (economic) abuse

Illegal or financial exploitation and/or control of funds and other resources needed for economic and personal survival. Forcing a person to be materially dependent.

Neglect

Wilful neglect

Refusal or failure to fulfil a caretaking obligation, including a conscious and intentional attempt to inflict physical or emotional stress, for example, deliberate abandonment or deliberate denial of food, money or health-related services.

Unwitting neglect

Failure to fulfil a caretaking obligation, excluding a conscious and intentional attempt to inflict physical or emotional distress, for example, abandonment, non-provision of food, money or health-related services because of anxiety, inadequate knowledge, laziness or infirmity.

Appendix II: Severity of maltreatment

From Browne and Herbert (1996).

Minor

Minor incidents with little or no long-term damage, either physical, sexual or psychological.

Physical

Injuries confined in area and limited to superficial tissues, including cases of light scratch marks, small slight bruising, minute burns and small welts.

Sexual

Inappropriate sexual touching, invitations and/or exhibitionism.

Emotional

Occasional verbal assaults, denigration, humiliation, scapegoating, confusing atmosphere.

Neglect

Occasional withholding of love and affection, weight parallel to or slightly below third centile with no organic cause.

Moderate

More frequent incidents and/or of a more serious nature, but unlikely to be life-threatening or have such potentially long-term effects.

Physical

Surface injuries of an extensive or more serious nature and small subcutaneous, including cases of extensive bruising, large welts, lacerations, small haematomas and minor burns.

Sexual

Non-penetrative inappropriate sexual interaction, such as fondling.

Emotional

Persistent verbal assaults, denigration and humiliation, occasional rejection.

Neglect

Persistent withholding of love and affection, non-organic growth, failure to gain weight.

Severe

Long-term, on-going abuse *or* less frequent incidents with potentially very severe physical or psychological harm.

Physical

All long and deep tissue injuries (including fractures, dislocations, subdural haematomas, serious burns and damage to internal organs).

Sexual

Sexual interaction involving attempted or actual oral, anal or vaginal penetration.

Emotional

Withholding of food and drink, enforced isolation and restriction of movement, persistent rejection.

Neglect

Persistent unavailability of parent or guardian, non-organic growth failure to gain weight and height.

Appendix III: Children's needs: ten child care commandments

The following guidelines appeared in a 1975 book called *The Needs of Children* by Mia Kellmer Pringle.

I. Give continuous, consistent, loving care – it's as essential for the mind's health as food is for the body.
2. Give generously of your time and understanding – playing with and reading to your child matters more than a tidy, smooth-running home.
3. Provide new experiences and bathe your child in language from birth onwards – they enrich a child's growing mind.
4. Encourage a child to play in every way both by him/herself and with other children – exploring, imitating, constructing, pretending and creating.
5. Give more praise for effort than for achievement.
6. Give a child ever-increasing responsibility – like all skills, it needs to be practised.
7. Remember that every child is unique – so suitable handling for one may not be right for another.
8. Make the way you show disapproval fit your child's temperament, age and understanding.
9. Never threaten that you will stop loving your child or give him/her away; you may reject the child's behaviour but never suggest that you might reject him/her.
10. Don't expect gratitude, your child did not ask to be born – the choice was yours.

Appendix IV: Responsiveness to the infant

Child's name:
Child's age:
Date:

Base your ratings, for the categories below, on a representative and fair sample of observations. Some working criteria of responsive parenting are provided below.

	Ratings			
Does the caregiver or parent:	Always	Most of the time	Some of the time	Never
Respond promptly to the infant's needs?				
Respond appropriately to his/her needs?				
Respond consistently?				
Interact smoothly and sensitively with the child?				

Prompt responding

Infants have very limited abilities to appreciate the contingencies (association) of events to their own behaviour; an interval of only three seconds is required to disrupt the contingency learning of six-month-old infants. Where the adult takes appreciably longer to answer the infant's signals there will be no opportunity for the child to learn that his/her behaviour can thereby affect his/her environment and in particular the behaviour of other people.

Appropriate responding

This means the ability to recognize the particular 'messages' the infant is trying to communicate, and to interpret and react to them correctly.

Consistency

A child's environment must be predictable; s/he must be able to learn that his/her behaviour will produce particular consequences under particular conditions.

Interacting smoothly

Parents can mesh their interactions with the infant's in a manner that is facilitative and pleasurable as opposed to intrusive and disruptive.

Appendix V: Parent–infant interaction

Child's name:
Child's age:
Date:

Does the parent:	Yes	No	Don't know
Initiate positive interactions with the infant?			
Respond to the infant's vocalizations?			
Change voice tone when talking to the infant?			
Show interest in face-to-face contact with the infant?			
Show the ability to console or comfort the infant?			
Enjoy close physical contact with the infant?			
Respond to the infant's indications of distress?			

Appendix VI: Quality of care (emotional needs)

Evaluate the quality of care in the boxes provided by rating it as Excellent (E), Good (G), Adequate (A), Poor (P), or Inadequate (I).

Emotional needs	Rating	Some defining criteria
1. Security	☐	Security means continuity of care, a predictable environment, consistent controls, settled patterns of care and daily routines, fair and understandable rules, harmonious family relationships, the feeling that one's home and family are always there.
2. Affection	☐	Affection includes physical contact, admiration, touching, holding, comforting, making allowances, being tender, showing concern, communicating.
3. Responsibility	☐	Responsibility involves discipline appropriate to the child's stage of development, providing a model to emulate/imitate, indicating limits, insisting on concern for others.
4. Independence	☐	Independence implies making opportunities for the child to do more unaided and to make decisions, first about small things but gradually about larger matters.
5. Responsiveness	☐	Responsiveness means prompt, consistent, appropriate actions to meet the child's needs.
6. Stimulation	☐	Stimulation means encouraging curiosity and exploratory behaviour, by praising, by responding to questions and play, by promoting training/educational opportunities and new experiences.

Appendix VII: Quality of physical care

Evaluate the quality of physical care in the boxes provided by rating it as Excellent (E), Good (G), Adequate (A), Poor (P), or Inadequate (I).

Physical needs	Rating	Some guiding questions
1. Shelter	☐	Does the child have reasonable accommodation (for example, a warm, dry bed; some privacy; a place for his/her property; a place to play)?
2. Food	☐	What, and how often, does the child eat and drink? Who usually feeds the child? What times are the meals? Are there problems feeding the child?
3. Safety	☐	Is the child protected from danger (for example, poisons/medicines locked away; training to avoid accidents, dangerous situations; children not left alone at night)?
4. Rest	☐	What time does the child go to bed? How much sleep does s/he get? Where does s/he sleep? Alone? Does s/he have difficulties in (a) sleeping? (b) staying in bed?
5. Cleanliness	☐	Is the child taught personal hygiene (for example, wash hands after toilet)? Are cuts and bruises attended to after a fall? Is the child encouraged to wash, bath, clean hair? Are they done for him/her? How often?
6. Appearance	☐	Is the child reasonably/appropriately clothed (for example, warm/tidy)? Does the child smell? Is s/he grubby?

Appendix VIII: Parental Care Checklist (school-age period)

Place a tick in the appropriate column.

Does the parent/caregiver:	Always	Usually	Some-times	Seldom	Never
1. Encourage the child's ideas?					
2. 'Listen' carefully so as to understand?					
3. Communicate clearly to the child?					
4. Respect his/her privacy?					
5. Set an example for the child?					
6. Provide guidance at appropriate times?					
7. Share (family news/appropriate decisions)?					
8. Respect the child's views?					
9. Acknowledge the child's efforts?					
10. Demonstrate emotional support (by comforting or encouraging)?					
11. Keep confidences?					
12. Make eye contact during conversation?					
13. Address the child by name?					
14. Remember the child's birthday?					
15. Talk to the child about family matters?					
16. Discuss (when appropriate) religion, politics, sex, education, death, etc.?					
17. Teach the child appropriate social skills?					
18. Accept the child's friends?					
19. Manage, resolve (fairly) any conflicts between children?					
20. Set reasonable limits and stick to them?					

Appendix IX: Health and Development Questionnaire

Ask caregiver/s:

1. Has … had any serious illnesses other than normal childhood illness?
2. Has s/he ever been in hospital? If so when? For what? For how long?
3. Does … have any current illness or disability? Is s/he attending a hospital, clinic or seeing a GP for this?
4. Does … currently (or in the past) have a problem with hearing or sight?
5. How would you describe …'s developmental progress and growth so far?
6. (a) What did … weigh at birth?
   (b) Did s/he gain weight quickly or slowly?
   (c) When did s/he double their birth weight?
7. At what age did … sit unaided?
8. At what age did … walk?
9. At what age did … talk? (Single words/sentences)
10. At what ages did … become clean and dry respectively (a) by day? (b) by night?
11. Does … have any problem at school either in relation to school work, general behaviour, attendance, or with friends? If so, describe it.
12. Does s/he seem to be different at school than at home?
13. What are the interests, hobbies, activities … most enjoys?
14. Does … make friends easily? Is s/he socially isolated?

Ask yourself:

15. Is the child's behaviour appropriate to his/her age, intelligence and social situation?
16. Is the environment making reasonable demands of the child?

17. Is the environment satisfying the crucial needs of the child, that is, the needs that are vital at his/her particular stage of development?

Note: You may need to seek the assistance of medical and health visitor colleagues to ensure that information about the child's growth and development is collated and properly interpreted. Health authorities have arrangements for children to have a developmental surveillance by a doctor or health visitor at specified intervals. Paediatricians stress the importance of monitoring children's growth by the regular use of weight and height charts and it is generally agreed that such charts should be kept for all young children.